SOME SLOW BEES

SOME SLOW BEES

Carol Potter

Oberlin College Press
Oberlin, Ohio

The FIELD Poetry Series, vol. 34
Oberlin College Press, 50 N. Professor Street, Oberlin, OH 44074
www.oberlin.edu/ocpress

Cover and book design: Steve Farkas
Cover image: Georgia O'Keeffe, "Red and Orange Streak" (1919, oil on canvas), Philadelphia Museum of Art. Bequest of Georgia O'Keeffe for the Alfred Steiglitz Collection, 1987. Reproduced by permission.

Library of Congress Cataloging-in-Publication Data

Potter, Carol, 1950-
  [Poems. Selections]
  Some slow bees / Carol Potter.
     pages ; cm. — (Field poetry series ; vol. 34)
  ISBN 978-0-932440-48-8 (softcover : acid-free paper) —
  ISBN 0-932440-48-7 (softcover : acid-free paper)
  I. Title.
  PS3566.O695A6 2015
  811'.54—dc23
                                        2014038527

In Memoriam: Jean Fenton Potter

Contents

I

M   *3*

The Good Pig   *4*

By What Sign?   *6*

Where She Came From   *8*

Busybody   *9*

Falling in Folds   *10*

The Secret Drinker   *16*

Baby Insomniac   *17*

Some Slow Bees   *19*

One Last Glimpse   *20*

It Goes   *21*

When Dogs Had Jobs   *22*

II

Are You Feeling It Yet?   *25*

Blockade   *26*

Cretins   *27*

Derelict   *28*

Enunciation   *29*

Fallow   *30*

Grunion   *31*

Hecklers   *32*

Ideogram   *33*

Jokes   *34*

Katydids   *35*

Lizards   *36*

Mouth   *37*

Nudes   *38*

Omniscience   *39*

Pancakes   *40*

Queered   *41*

Roses   *42*

Sugar   *43*
Twinkies   *44*
Uranium   *45*
Voodoo   *46*
Welcome   *47*
X-ray   *48*
Yo-yo   *49*
Zippo   *50*

III
Tats   *53*
I Would Be Smoking   *55*
4th of July   *56*
Sticky Fingers   *57*
Fungible Facts   *58*
A Kind of Ruffling Course in the World   *59*
Distant Buffaloes   *60*
4444   *61*
Does That White Seem Cold?   *62*
DNA   *63*
Dreaming of Disguise   *64*
Auction   *65*
Silage   *66*
Plank by Plank   *67*
Tuck & Roll   *68*
Spikehorn   *69*

IV
The Miss Nancy Papers   *73*

Acknowledgments   *83*

Every story has its chapter in the desert, the long slide from kingdom
to kingdom through the wilderness,
where you learn things, where you're left to your own devices.

—Richard Siken, "Driving, Not Washing"

I

M

Last week's flood took out
the blue railroad bridge north of here.
Watered two schools. I pictured
the darkened smudge nudging its way
into classrooms, first graders
at their desks the first week
of school forming their letters.
The curious humps of n's and m's.
Yellow coats in motorboats
hovering outside the windows,
waving to them, "Hello! Hello!"
the children think. It's nothing
strange to them. The odd behavior
of adults. Nothing to be alarmed about.
"What a world," they mutter to themselves.
Smell of yellow paper and dark pencil.
Mountains of m's on their pages.
Water trickling under the door.
Really, there's nothing strange about it.
This flood at their feet.
That man in the red checked shirt
and blue hat jumping up and down
in his boat waving his arms.
Who knows what he wants?

The Good Pig

Might have been the books we read as children,
our confusion about human protocol. Who calls whom.

What to do now, etc. All those animals dressed
in human clothes. The kid with the animal snout and

beaver teeth, fur all over his body but dressed
in blue overalls. Droopy donkey and humming

fat bear. Everybody chatting one to the other.
Bad bunny. Jealous bear sister. Maybe

it was the chamomile in B. Potter's books.
Something about McGregor. We picked up

some odd ideas. About getting caught
under the flower pot. Losing your shoes.

Leaving your coat behind on the fence.
One reasonable lesson after the other and everything

ending well. Don't lie down in that bed.
Don't eat that porridge. Don't knock on that door.

In the story, supper gets delivered to the table.
You were bad and you were almost eaten

but there you are at last in the little burrow
with the fires burning. A bit of fur missing.

Some shame. Mother, however,
seems to have forgiven you.

Or let's say, your house blown down,
but the wolf's in the pot. Everybody huddling

in the smartest pig's house. The good pig.
And out the window Thomas the Train passing by.

Smile on his face. Always pleasant.
Some furry hands waving from the windows.

By What Sign?

If you could just say I feel lost here and I'm going to go home now. For where on earth would you buy that ticket. Who would meet you when you got there. By what sign would they know you.

—C. D. Wright, *One Big Self*

Yes, you could wonder by which sign
they would know you. It could be simply
which side of the door you happened to be
standing on and how long you were there.
Maybe the sunlight is reflecting in such a
way as to give you a beard when
you have no beard. Dust in the wind
has coated your eyelids. Who could
recognize you? If it could be simple like
that. Just a matter of time of day.
Whether the wind was blowing or not.
Or sugar on your face and bees
coming in to sup. Who would know you
with all those wings at your lips?
Like the cats yesterday, bedmates
for two years then staring at each other
from opposite sides of the glass door,
and both of them terrified. The female
did not know the male because she was
outside looking in and she'd never
been there before. He was seeing
a cat where usually there was none.
They reared up and started hissing at each other,
batting the glass door between them and when
she came in, they went on fighting.
Slips of grass draped across her back, rose petals
sticking to her fur. The wet of snail on her pads.
A simple trick of light. And those snails

she had been investigating?
Nothing any of us in this house know
the first thing about. They crawl up to the door
at night. Cling to the side of the house.
In the morning you can see where they've been.
The wet trail drying out in the sun like thin glue.
A slight stain on the walk.

Where She Came From

after Jonathan Edwards

we wouldn't expect to find one human-shaped mound or anything
do not look back or stop anywhere in the valley
notwithstanding all the special warnings and messages
graceless, godless, impenitent, and unbelieving

do not look back or stop anywhere in the valley
the world was in her heart
graceless, godless, impenitent, and unbelieving
the smoke of the land went up like the smoke of a furnace

do not look back or stop anywhere in the valley
her heart was in the world
the smoke of the land went up like the smoke of a furnace
one that stands or walks in slippery places is always exposed to fall

her heart was in the world
notwithstanding all her special warnings and messages
one that stands or walks in slippery places is always exposed to fall
we wouldn't expect to find one human-shaped mound or anything.

Busybody

We were happy in the attic, nothing onerous
about what we were doing. There was a bed
that needed to be made, and a turban grandfather
had brought back from his job in the middle east.
We wore the turban, and wrapped some kind of
sashes around our waists because we were
tomboys. We were extraterrestrials. We were
tanned hardy men. We made a pact to not be girls.
To save ourselves. If there had been some kind
of serum perhaps. If we could have been
deported from the country we found ourselves
in. That was the plan. Sailors smoking opium on deck,
wassailing everybody straight out of port,
dolphins leaping across the bow. No lawns. No
piglets. No possums. No boobs. No busybodies.
We did not have the sense there was anything irregular about this.
We were the sons. We were rude and
fancied ourselves renegades, teasing the meek.
I was an ace at it. A comma between
my legs and egress everywhere I looked.
In Home Ec., I flattened cakes on purpose.
Banged pots. Ripped seams. Back when
you had to take that course if you were a girl.
If you had what I had. Irrelevant what I wrought
in that class. I let spools of thread out windows.
I tossed eggs out onto the roof.
You could see them there for a long time,
the spent shells, the smoking yolks.
All accolades were belated.

Falling in Folds

1.

I lived in a house but have left a house behind.
As in put all the books into a box.
I put it in a truck. I took a cab.
I drove away from the pond
in which we swam summers.
In the pond children were floating
on giant tractor tubes. I was
in the crowd, there on the pond,
but then I left it.
Left the children and the old mother
in a muslin dress and father
at the edge of the water. Father
fishing even though he could barely
walk; the children's cries
from the inner tubes seemed to be
buffeting the old man's face
as I waved goodbye.

2.

I was in the crowd all along,
but needed to get out of there.
We had immersed ourselves
in the works of an incorruptible author.
We were studying hard and then saw
there was nothing going to be coming
out of it as in something was in and
now it is out. As in the end of the world
had come and we had been there,

but then it started up again.
Like some kind of crease in the sky
the way a cloud lingers long after dark
and you're just not sure.

3.

In a linen shirt, in mourning
for the house I had been in,
I felt like I was blind in one eye.
Not one in a hundred would have
done what I did. I was not
in the army nor was I in politics.
I was in clover in brown boots
in hot water in love.
I was in trouble there.

4.

In reply to your inquiry,
we had gone off in honor
of the migration
in itself absolutely.
We took to crossing rivers.
Sometimes we were packed
in dozens ready to be sold
in building plots. All of us
in loco parentis, falling
in folds. No one thought
we had it in us in any case;
insofar as you could put it
in your pocket
cut it in half
throw it in the fire.

5.

I was in flagrante delicto
in the middle of her many
limbs later. I was in her hands
and she was rubbing me
up and down. My hair
in her face; I was on end
while she loved me,
then she got in her truck,
drove west. I stood on the curb
in full sunlight inside the state
of Indiana. Crabapples fallen
on the sidewalk around me.
The sound of bees inside everything.

6.

Weak in algebra
though never wanting in courage,
I trust
in her. She will be
in my face.
In media res.
In the box.
In the middle of her body.
In the midst of her.
In the center.

7.

As in a change in the constitution.
Seven in number, four feet in width.
In fact
in truth
in any case

insofar as she may come in.
When she comes in
lock her in.
Let her be in.
I will throw in the harness.
I will wear the coat
with the green side
in nearest the body.
I will go
into the thick of it.

8.

We were in the situation.
The who did what
to which woman
and where will we be then?
We are within something
and we enjoy feeling the soft edge of it around us,
pressing our hands
to the skin
at the edge of this place
in which we are
in, the smooth elastic rim
of this world.

9.

In ancient times
they would not speak of this.
Though this is what they did.
Including themselves in each other.
In time one would forget
to omit the other
as in indicating inclusion
within time.

Though they included each other in ancient times
they might have known enough
to speak in a whisper.
To indicate limitation.
And to be similar in appearance
to the ones in charge
so as not to cause alarm
and exclude each other by accident.
In extremis.

10.

We were told to speak in French,
to indicate some means.
To indicate motion or direction
from outside to a point within.
Let's go inside the house we said to each other.
I wanted her to point everything within.
To come inside. To go back
in the house with me. To be in me
and to include me
within her means
without limitation.
I asked her to lie
down then on top of me
so we could break in half
at that moment so we could move
from one condition to another.

11.

Speaking in honor
of being in with her,
and on top of her in the right moment.
We break in half with the skin media res

in the middle of each other.
Speaking of each other to indicate object
or purpose I indicated to her
with my skin to lie down with me,
to be inside me and include me
to that point within the transition.
We were in the same position some
times, but often changing positions.
We could not believe our good fortune
to be so often on the inside
of each other and to have it in.
Because she did do that
and did it over and over
we were engaged in it,
we were rejoicing in it.
We were speaking
in that way to indicate motion.

12.

She is there in the middle of it
and she is breaking in half
and it is not like grief when someone dies
because the dead just go ahead
and stay where they were put.
Which is a good thing. She is there
in longing and in another place
altogether so as to indicate inclusion
and the smallest place in her grows
large going from the outside
to the inside and back out again.
Here in this place where one waits
for the other as in the word, incused,
as in one has printed something
inside the other.

The Secret Drinker

When I heard the woman in the next booth say that her mother
had been a secret drinker, I thought about what the mother
might have liked to drink, and why we assume it was something bad for her.
If you made it two nouns instead of a noun and its adjective,
you could tell yourself she was simply drinking a secret,
as in swallowing something down she didn't want to tell.
I was sitting with my mother eating Ginger Chicken String Beans,
and when I looked up at the dark TV screen above the door,
it looked like there were two doors out of the place but one door
was just a reflection, refracting and doubling on the screen.
I was pleased by the illusion. Neither door was where the real one
actually was. There was an exit where there might not be one.
It was one of those strip mall restaurants. Horizontal mirror 7 feet long,
rimmed by a picture of a waterfall in China I most likely will never see.
The cook and the waitress were chatting in Chinese, and my mother
was forgetting what she thought she might have been saying. I was trying
to think up questions to ask her but I was contemplating secret drinking
and where that woman's mother went to do it.
I pictured a shed behind a house not far from here; a woman sitting
at a window watching snow fall. The quiet thing snow does
shifting towards us, filling up a yard. The woman is putting her lips
to the rim of a glass she has hidden behind the garden forks.
She is sucking the secret drink into her body. It is like one of those
long worms they drag from the sand. It keeps coming and coming.
It is elastic. You can pull and pull on it and it won't break. I wanted to know
how no one knew she was back there drinking in secret.
Why no one put their faces to her mouth to smell that room
at her lips. Bicycle grease on her knees. Those tulips wintering over.
"I'll be right back," she might have said before she left the room.
"Does anyone want anything from the fridge?" she might have
added, closing the door softly behind her.

Baby Insomniac

Of course baby sits up at night because baby
having been here in some other form previously
knows that the sun is up in the other world
and there's no telling what might happen.

Baby's got rabbit ears on, little antenna in her
heart that knows if she doesn't make some
noise in the dark, there won't be any sounds
but the parents asleep in the other room, stirring and

snoring and rifling through their dreams.
One needs to keep watch
and this baby knows it. She sits up and
picks at the bars of the crib. At the little

play mobile they rigged, the bright danglers
that are supposed to entertain her, assuage her,
keep her from wanting to pull herself over the side
of the crib and crawl off somewhere else.

What to do about the restlessness of babies,
the way they pick at loose flecks of paint,
the way they put anything in the mouth,
as if they know they'll be needing

some grit in their gullets? Some ballast.
Like what turkeys have
in their gizzards. Something in there
to grind up what they swallow.

Of course baby sits up at night
staring at the dark
as it moves itself shape by shape.
Then the moon coming in,

shifting its way around the room
as if looking for the baby there,
big eyes shining; soft spot like a tent flap—
little scrap of hair on top.

Some Slow Bees

a landscape a person
could graze in   could walk outside
eat so much green and the apples
you would need to know how to climb
how to swing up into the branches
avoid the yellow jackets clustered on the fruit

*

green apples falling into the yard
bees eating them if you can say that bees eat
gouges in the apples
4-5 bees in each gouge   the sap loosened
sweet all over the ground
the grass has a throat of sweet and it's humming around your feet
put some shoes on I tell you
the mound of apples in the rake and the bees unnerved
fruit falling as we speak
we can't keep up with it the apples
that red bird singing

*

napkin thrown down on the floor
an ending of sorts Saturday dinner on the table
walking out each door you in your socks out front
zucchini with the knife stuck in it
who said what to whom
me in the chair out back the stars I stared up at
I keep thinking I ought to know their names
been looking at them my whole life ought to be able to discern
Big Dipper from little shield of Achilles from dog of the world
in the corner of the yard
sweet stink of apples in the dark and the bees that eat them

One Last Glimpse

The god of your childhood likes it when you make mistakes
    you can't undo. And the way we like to think everything's

for the better. It's an American trait. We shout and clap
    for each other: "Go on. Go ahead," we say. "You first!"

But there you have Lot's wife taking that one last glimpse
    and turning herself into salt. Meanwhile Lot runs on ahead

just glad to get out of the burning valley. Perhaps god is amused
    to see you down in the valley later trying to determine

which is Lot's wife and which is one of the Sodomites.
    There you are tasting those pillars with your tongue.

Seeing which is salt. Which is chalk. "Tastes like soap to me!"
    you shout, white paste on your tongue you can't get rid of.

It Goes

Too much metaphor in your life might mean you need
    to be talking about something but you'd rather not.

You've given yourself a gag order. You're trying
    not to let your left hand see what your right hand

is doing. Waving at passing boats. Locking your
    bicycle to the pylon on the pier. Forgetting about the tide.

How the plank to land is horizontal at 9 PM.
    Almost vertical at 6 AM and the crabs scuttling along the rocks

in full sunlight. It's like forgetting about death
    but without the like. Tide going down

and pulling the bicycle down to the pier. You come out
    next morning and there's your bicycle flattened

like in some kind of terrible headlock.
    Cable dragged down below the dock.

Frame bent, the gear shift mechanism ground off.
    You like thinking there's something you can do about

almost anything; that there's nothing really wrong
    with the bike. Just a bit of tilt to the right

and the wheel out of round. That peculiar
    thumping sound everywhere you go,

"But, hey," you tell yourself,
    "It goes."

When Dogs Had Jobs

All entreated the moon and stars for help. Palatial observatories were founded at Paris, London, and Berlin for the express purpose of determining longitude by the heavens.

—Dava Sobel, *Longitude*

According to Sobel, lesser minds devised
navigational schemes that depended
on the yelps of wounded dogs strategically

anchored on the open ocean, but how would
one have known if the dog yelping
was the dog you were supposed to be listening to,

or just some random dog getting hit by its master for
failing to chase the sheep it should have chased?
This was back when dogs worked. When they had

jobs to do. And there you are out on the sea
when the fog comes in and you can't tell
which is which. The dog anchored off Point Ives,

or the dog off in some field getting punished?
You're ringing the bell. You hear your own heart
tipping itself back and forth like a buoy. You can't see

your hand in front of your face. You're a long way
from home, or you're closer than you thought.
No sense asking yourself why you got on the boat

in the first place, why this particular boat, and why today?
The barking you were depending on is getting
softer and softer as you drift in the fog.

Nothing else out there, but the sound of
something far off pitching and yawing.
Someone moving around on an open deck, maybe.

II

Are You Feeling It Yet?

When Ajax, hippie dog that he was, chased
the train at the end of our block

it was the end of Ajax. We were hippies & we went on
being hippies, glad to let anything run free.

We left the doors ajar; anybody
could walk in when anybody wanted. All being

in obvious disrepair we were running amok
half the time. Are you feeling it yet?

We grew up, grew more attentive as children
came & went to war again. What more might we be asked

to adopt we'd like to know, the next generation angry just
some of the time, & the rest simply astrological.

That dog never adapted to the world with the tracks
laid out & the trains arriving on time. I haven't owned a dog since.

Blockade

Bequeath to the second one what
the brainy one pushed around on her

plate. This was her favorite food but she would not eat.
She got up from the table bragging she was done

with us. She had wanted the brass
bell grandmother had promised,

but was given the silver blade instead.
Carried it in her shoulder bag all day long.

I liked her black moods & went with her to the house. We stood
on the stoop ringing the buzzer; no one

was home but the old woman without a leg.
Blockade the rest of it from memory,

if you don't mind. How the brain
avails itself of its own little blight,

erasing those fabulous balloons of back-story
one by one. Birds singing in the eaves,

& the nearly blind woman with one leg
beginning her slow progress across the floor.

Cretins

Cold as in not cordial, she had completely
mastered the quick check to the eye. She was

trying to forget those crenulations in her character
she was embarrassed about. "Chop Suey,"

she replied to everything. Even the names
of her children. Their faces confused her,

gave her no comfort. "I'm calling the cops,"
she yelled when they confiscated the keys to her

convertible. Nothing can protect you
from that. From mother caught blind, driving the white line

on the road, trying to converse with friends huddled
in the back seat. "Too many cretins

all around," she told the children
congregating above her bed watching her

as if the curtain of her face were a compass & one might
cultivate a piece of north & south there, something west.

Derelict

Disgruntled winds were puffing the sand
along the desert floor driven vertically

into the windshield. She was trying to smoke some dope
in that wind, but the embers kept dogging her

into the car, forcing her to lie down on the back seat.
She was delayed, stuck by the side of the road waiting.

Daylight went by as she dallied, revising the story.
She wanted a drink but there was nothing in the car, nothing

by the side of the road. Derelict in all her duties, just
sitting there by the road dutiful to the dirt, to the sound of the

dust flicking by & everything done that could be done.
She thought of singing but this was the desert after all,

sand drilling towards her, and the song
more of a dirge than a ditty.

Enunciation

Eduardo chats in Spanish on his cell phone
in the next berth, our elegant boats hull to hull

& his boyfriend, 20 years younger, ecstatic sometimes, but more often
in trouble. Perhaps exotic, living on a boat,

hunkered down in the V berth at night, engine tuned, tank full,
sails ready to unfurl at next light. It's an expensive life & what I have

been spending, I don't want to add up. A form of euthanasia
really, how a person can clude her former self.

Walk away easy as getting into any car & driving
but then there you are. At an elevation you've

never experienced before, eels dangling
at the ends of rods & you just glad to see

something you've never seen before. Everybody likes
hearing of someone slipping the knot as if it were European,

& something sophisticated but enough is enough you might
tell yourself carefully easing the boat out of the berth, your ears

burning. My mother taught me to enunciate, not to eat
with my mouth full. Everything else I did myself.

Fallow

Farm what you want. You have your cows,
your chickens, your farmer's daughters. They say there's

something wholesome about all this, fair game
everywhere; daughter plucking eggs from the chickens,

& the faulted eggs left to rot. Hold them to the light, then
fast as you can, drop them. Though she was

a farm girl, she was no fox; nonetheless
she'd seen plenty of fucking in her time.

It was Faulknerian, big muddy boots
everywhere the family went

& too much fat at the top of the milk, no barns burned down
but almost. Milk faucet left open now & again,

& the whole tank emptied. Fascist they sometimes called their
father, but they loved him in the end.

Finally, after he died, the brothers
who'd inherited the farm took to fighting

over the upper 40 which had long since gone fallow,
all the cows sold off & nobody speaking. Fulsome as

farming seems at first, it can leave
a person thirsty, the last family farm in America

packed up, & mother in the old folks' home
seemingly unfazed, singing into her soup: "Que Sera, Sera."

Grunion

Perfect teeth but lots of gripes about mother
& father rich as they were; the way gruff dad

would grip the kids, take them on the town
but forget them. "Saddle up, men," he'd guffaw

& off he'd go only to leave them at some
greasy corner looking for another way home. It's a cliché perhaps.

The poor little rich kids & drunk daddy gone for
good & all of it public.

Where there were grackles it turns
out there were geese; where the lovers went

to watch grunion run, there was only a
green boat bobbing & nobody in it.

You should suspect the grail that any one story grows to be,
the way lovers tell each other the get-

go of their lives; after it's over, you find
yourself one of the characters gaslighted,

& that grimace on your face
as if god herself had

given you a mouth full of
grass, some grit to eat.

Hecklers

Herons were feeding at the water's edge
beneath scores of helium balloons

caught in branches rubbing on each other. Hull to
hull the boats gleamed &

bobbed after the rainstorm, gulls haranguing each other
at the top of each mast. Heave the sail up,

& set it loose. Honor thy father & mother they say,
but there's no one at the helm any longer.

The hearts went out on us after. Remove the
hecklers from the street; put them back

in their houses. Hell sticks its fingers up.
How many can you see now?

Hold that thought. Count backwards by seven.

Ideogram

I was feeling alone there & then I felt more so.
Her name was Irene. We were, as so many

people are, inadvertently together. On my
shoulder, the ideogram for the one who incensed

Irene over & over. Something inexhaustible
in the way I looked at the door groping for something

appropriate to say. Indicate if you get what I mean,
but no matter what I did, I managed to ignite her.

I am no dope & it was easy to identify the idea
as it itched itself to the surface. The sky was

the color of iron when I drove to the boat,
opened the hatch. I would have inserted a finger

into that hole she kept making but that story about Hans
& the dike is just a myth. Sometimes the rise of water

is imperceptible; one minute you have a street,
the next, a river. Which is why in every idyll you need

a flock of iridescent sails unfurling, some swarthy sailors
shouting across indigo seas.

I had a place to go to,
& I went.

Jokes

Jill's baby cried 3 hours every night
& jack-all she could do about it. She rocked

baby & sang to baby but just as soon as baby
was quiet, baby would jazz up again. She tried

to joke with baby but babies don't get jokes.
If babies got jokes, babies would know how to

swim when they jigged their way into the world.
They'd know how to drive, how to juice their own baby dinners.

Mash their own pears. They'd jettison themselves up
onto counters, jimmy the cupboards open.

They'd know how to forage like other juvenile animals.
None of this lying around waiting for Jean or Jim or

Jerry to pick them up, they'd be
jury-rigging their cribs when the rain

started to fall, making jib sails out of
diapers. Jesting all the time. Never out

of joint. One knock-knock
joke after the other.

Katydids

"Kiss the day goodbye," the record player sang.
Something slightly kinky about the setting. Those dance lessons

I gave Karen & Kitty, then removed them from the class
because it seemed out of kilter, the makeup, the little

sparkly dresses, the town. I would give a kidney
to either of my girls if I had to; god knows

I didn't kit them out very well, constantly in debt
& all three of us slightly unkeeled. No matter, I would go

back to it, that little kennel of a house, katydids
singing in the grass like massive karaoke machines

& the children at the kitchen table pretending
they knew all the words to the songs; my two girls

knocking out the tunes,
knowing what they knew & going on with it.

Lizards

Lesbians, they say, have it easy but it's a
marriage like any other marriage. "Love it,"

she told me, but I didn't. I went lunging
across the irrigated lawn, no

longer wanting to be lugubrious about anything.
I sent the letter to one thinking it was

the other & now I'd like to be leaving this corner in the wind.
Leaks spring in the heart, in the head, in the lungs.

I would lay it down in the sand on the corner
but my hand touches leather when I feel inside it. I won't forget

her lips on mine, nor what we promised each other.
There were no locusts in this story. There were fires

on the mountains. Lizards running along the tops of the walls;
a landscape neither of us knew how to keep.

Mouth

Mother knows we're all made of different
metals, though none of us murderers as far as I know.

However it's the little murders that matter. The fear
when masturbating perhaps. Never mingle

business with pleasure & therefore most of us
muffle our cries while making love.

When we swore she marched us to the bathroom,
washed our mouths out with soap. We liked

our dinners on time but never liked mustard
on hot dogs; how quickly we stuffed them

in our mouths, mangled each one.
We were hungry & there were too many of us.

Miss each other? Not that much. Too many elbows
& knees caked with mud. Too many mouths

at the table, mumbling. Some things went the wrong way
& there's no music can repair it. Though you can

make it melodious, like one of those folk songs
about something monstrous, but the voice so sweet

and the tune so mellifluous, nobody
seems to mind the words.

Nudes

Nudes don't make it here & neither does
nice & we know it trying to nudge each other

outside to check on the dogs, nipples erect,
our fingers numb from that cold front

sliding north. I was on the lawn waving back
at you playing your fiddle at the window, but nothing I did

could make you come to the door. I was suddenly nauseated
by the smell of nutmeg wafting from the kitchen

as if something normal was going on but we're not
normal & never meant to be I suppose.

Neither of us had much to say at the end. It reminded me
of that new math we had during Sputnik,

trying to add it all up but finally just nodding
& shaking & nothing to show for all those figures,

rows of numbers blurring across the page
& everybody suddenly really nervous.

Omniscience

Octagonal houses were lit up against the sky.
I was trying my best to orient myself east

by northwest but I went on being obtuse.
I was stumped by the glass panes at sunset. One could confuse

the red glass for fires, for some old trouble coming back at you,
for a certain loss of direction. Omniscience isn't all that much fun really.

Too many obstacles you see before you get there,
but you go anyway. Onionskin pages flipped

in the wind of that sunset; orthodox
Christians stood on the hilltop praying for the end.

Orioles sang in the high trees, some sweet tune
in spite of the ornery way the world seemed to have turned.

Pancakes

Perhaps it was Bing Crosby pulling himself
across the floor naked except for a diaper prompted that response

from me. There were pregnant cottonmouths in the river
below the house & one lone man with a pike in his hands

trying to kill the snakes. I had promised not to watch but couldn't help it.
Peeved by that vision, I drove to town.

It was not only my perception that things had gone too far.
I was sitting in traffic getting prodded by the SUV in back of me.

But this isn't what precipitated my response, nor the helicopters
proctoring from the sky. There was trouble & I couldn't tell where it was.

Just the choppers & a spotted pig on a leash next to a woman
holding a sign: "Pecker Heads, Go Back Where You Come From."

I was pickled at that point with angst, feeling
pugilistic. The image of Bing holding pancakes

in his mouth as he crawled toward me made me pine
for my previous life, the one where the sun doesn't shine so much.

Queered

Queer sight & hindsight have little to do with that quiz
she takes at night. She gave up quotidian. She queered her life.

Here's the quandary really. Being everyone's version of adventure.
You can quip about it. Joke around a bit.

Take a level bead on yourself. Quacks
won't help. It's your own little quagmire you find yourself in.

They were end to end quarreling with each other.
Call it hate if you want. How vengeful even the quake seemed,

shaking them like bad brats. Fifty-six years of that particular quest
had made her feel like quitting. Nothing you could do

to quiet that breaking window, those pieces crackling to the floor
& the quick white dog yipping under the bed as if he'd been

quilled, but it was the desert. No porcupines. Just two
women, a dog, & everybody queasy.

Roses

Risked the skin on the hand to take care
of the raccoon family we discovered living

in the walls of the house. Each morning resurrecting themselves,
they sang behind the framed pictures, rocking their

coonskin caps. Little radicals. I could have
radiated the house to get rid of them, drawn a

large red ring around the yard & bombed them out,
but it was a fair race in the end. I let them alone. I wore

rubber gloves when I slept to keep them from
nibbling my fingers. Kept a rack of cages to

catch them but could not bring myself to do it.
Reeds grew tall around the house & when I went outside

to rake up their droppings, their candy wrappers & chicken bones,
I saw how ridiculous I was which is something a person should

rarely see, or how else get up & go on to the next project—
Resuscitating birds. Ripping out roses. What have you.

Sugar

Shame on you, you might say to yourself,
letting that mistake snake its way through you.

Of course you didn't mean to slide
through that door. She called you

sugar, she called you
the best thing that ever happened to her,

but self-preservation doesn't always include us in it.
Sore as we might get sometimes,

we go on with it. Sick, you might think
but you married your own mother anyway.

Somnolence can take us through a few years, but
succulent as the table looks, don't sit down

just because you were invited. Surfeit yourself
on some air. Some blue birds in the sky,

a blast of wind. Souls are out there
looking for some lessons. Solitary

confinement isn't half as interesting to any of us
as Snow White dancing, her shiny black

shoes clacking beneath her as if she were trying
to run somewhere but she wasn't sure where.

Twinkies

Teacher saw it in you in the first place, your
refusal to work with the team you were assigned.

Had to get up move to another table,
tinker with the rubber glue. Punished, you wept

into the crook of your arm, a thimbleful, or two,
your throat opening & closing but you were already making

nefarious plans. Twisting in your seat, you imagined
giant fish eating the identical twins staring at you.

Every day their mother packed Twinkies in their lunch pails
neat & tidy & of course you tailed them around the yard

but they refused to give up those treats.
Teacher tied you into a chair when someone told

what you did. You remember her tepid breath
on your face, tips of her cool fingers setting your head down

on the desk, something almost tender in her touch,
that little dimple at the back of your neck tingling.

Uranium

Uncanny how we knew what to do at first
& suddenly we came undone

as we sat staring at each other & the sky united itself above us,
one cloud at a time disappearing from the upper parts

where supposedly someone thinks about ontology. Upholstery
had come loose from itself, & the children were eating uranium

to make themselves strong. Who were we to utter those words
of warning or to heed them? "Use me well," she whispered

into my ears & I tried, I tried, but we were being ushered
into a theater where the seats glowed & the screen looked slightly uterine

with nothing growing inside it. We watched the movie unaware
that we'd seen it ten times already. How could we be so unconscious

one might wonder? We tried to understand the directions,
urging each other on at every juncture: "Go ahead, it'll be good for you."

Voodoo

Ventriloquists won't do what needs to be done.
I was already tired of that particular venue & they were

tired of me. I took up the lines, went with vengeance in my heart
up the coast. When I came to a large vine-covered harbor,

I got out of the boat & asked the people the name of the village
but no one there knew what they called themselves. Such a view they had

& the trees on the bluff bending in a vigorous wind.
The harbor smelled like vinegar because the villagers were making

bad wine & drinking it as well. I had been searching for vegetables
to take on the next leg of my venture but came back with nothing

to find three villagers sleeping in the velvet berth.
My anger left me valence by valence, that vulgar

vintage staining their mouths, how could they help it?
I could have vacated that town then & there

but someone on the dock started playing her violin,
one voluptuous note after another, & I tell you

it came on me like voodoo, what I volunteered to do next
of my own volition, one vowel at a time.

Welcome

Wearing out one's welcome was a sin to avoid
Mother warned me consistently. Everywhere

I went I worried over my welcome, that spot of ground
my feet worked on & worked on as if they were

going to wear out the earth beneath me.
When I was 16, my friend's mother told me

I was not welcome at her daughter's party
& had never been invited. We should

watch for it, a certain restlessness in the host
that sufficiently wary folk will detect. You can hear it

in their voices. Mother walks up & down halls of her new
"home" having weathered the move

from her house, the death of my father. Word has it her sight
& most of her mind are gone, but whenever you ask how she's doing

she says it's nothing to worry about, "Blue Skies, Nothing but
Blue Skies," she warbles into the phone.

Whatever she does, she does nimbly.

X-ray

X-rayed over & over I thought I knew the story
but one of the ex-lovers came along with another version.

I would have xxxed her name
off the list & pretended I had never learned that x=y,

that xeroxed formula many seemed to be following.
X marks the spot where we lay down, the palo

verde bushes xanthic & both of us sneezing.
At Xmas, I gave her the xylophone to play

but she was tired of my xyloid efforts. I tried everything
I knew to live in that xeric climate but it turns out

I am not so good in such a dry world. Too many xenolites
in one place; something xenophobic

about the situation, & all around xanthoxylum
bushes flowering. Something fragrant the desert cannot X.

Yo-yo

The bright yolk of the sun broke over them; they
waded in yellow light: wild lemon trees

blossoming on the street, coyotes yowling
at the top of the arroyo. Three years in the desert

& neither could give up yearning for something the other
might yield. You don't need to know the whole

story; the wind kept kicking up, knocking the yucca
plants over, the whole yard tricking itself up & down

like a yo-yo in the hand of a small child, one sharp
yank, the string playing out & staying there.

Zippo

Zealot for loss you might think, as if there
were some virtue in it, as if Zeus, or if you will, god, enjoys

seeing you float like some zeppelin over a playground, the shadow
falling on the kids upside down zoning out on the swings & the monkey bars

as if the world were a zoo & they just needed to practice some
handholds. There's nothing zany about it. One last look at the dog

you're leaving behind. Make a zombie of the heart. Pack it up.
There's no story we can't tell ourselves. Zigzag between blocks as you

drive away. See those palms zippering the sky, those tall straight
trunks black on blue. Zip it up, that lip.

Zinc your nose for the duration. That brilliant
sun zeroing in on your face. This is the desert.

The light like a massive Zippo lit but no concert hall full of
zapped-out kids waving their arms.

III

smart chickens, rickety world…
—Charles Simic

Tats

In truth I don't understand the etiquette of tattoos.
What I'm supposed to do around them. Study them
or pretend I don't see? Like love bites. The way
we don't stare at a stranger's hickey. The way we
wouldn't think to mention it. To study someone's
skin like that. The nurse in the office last week
with a story on each arm, something drawn elbow
to wrist but in a glance I had no idea what it was.
He took my blood pressure. Asked me questions
about my mood. My mother's failing heart. My job.
Something you can see in the bed with someone.
Skin to skin. Reaching behind a student yesterday,
her shoulders exposed though it's January,
I saw she had words written on her upper back,
several lines of script shoulder to shoulder, and
a little splash of some kind of drawing, but I
pretended I hadn't seen anything. Not appropriate
to study a young woman's exposed flesh. The
stud in her tongue flashing at me each time she said
the word stuck. She was stuck on some problem
she'd been having in English. The stud like something
bobbing in the ocean. You're not sure you see it, then
you do. Then you don't. The places we aren't
supposed to look. Trained as we are to avert
the eyes. As if only for the lover turning
the naked body in his or her arms to study the
colors. The writing and drawing. Not to be salacious.
Caught staring. What's the protocol? Public or private?
The intimacy of the writing there. Those pretty
pictures on the calf. The bicep. Top of the ass.
There's a promise. You could read the person
if you could only take the person into your arms.

You could study the script on her, the pictures.
Like reading any code. The way we look into a lover's eyes
as if to see the story there at the back of the pupil
talking to us. The way we put our mouth
on the lover's mouth as if to breathe in what
the person has inside there so you could know.
It is the act of knowing. It is the Adam and Eve
of it. The apple on the tree. The promise
that somehow we could start naming what this is.
What we do together here.

I Would Be Smoking

Bright moon in the desert, and that one bird
singing in the dark. Cars at the bottom of the hill.
First the stop light. Music somewhere, someone
dancing in a room. Someone breathing into someone
else's arms someplace in the city, a woman
turning in her bed, and the snails that climb
out of the blue flowers at night crawling
across the sidewalk. When I come outside,
I see them there with their heads out of
their shells and the long trail of slow wet behind them.
I came outside tonight and stood in the moonlight.
We had quarreled and she was sleeping in the bed.
Both of us disappointed, but one sleeping if you
could call what she was doing sleeping.
What love does to us sometimes if this is love.
What we said to each other. How it picks us
up out of the bed and makes us walk outside while
the other sleeps. One is always asleep and one
awake it seems. Outside on the patio,
I would smoke a cigarette if I were to smoke.
I would smoke it inside out, the lit end
inside the mouth to keep the smoking secret.
Unless of course the cheeks light up
the way children put flashlights in the mouth
to show the veins in their cheeks. You make
the whole mouth a giant pink balloon in the dark.
If we were children. If I was still smoking.

4th of July

When I saw the child weeping on the bus on the way back
from the fireworks her sister beside her father clinging
to the strap above them bus packed all of us tired having
just come from the waterfront those bombs bursting above
our heads cranked backwards to the sky when I saw how
quietly she was weeping her chest rising and falling that
slight sniffle stuffing it down I wondered how is it one
learns to do that silent weeping in a crowded bus the almost
imperceptible huff of her chest Dad going on with his
standing sister sitting quietly beside her when her eyes
briefly met mine she took her skinny bare legs folded
them up under her the way you would fold a shirt then
turned rolling her shoulders her chest her legs away
from all of us so she could stare out the black window
no one see her face one might wonder why we learn
to do that turn away from people stick ourselves into our
own sorrow leg by leg by arm gather it back into the body
whatever the grief is this girl seemed too small to have
learned that yet too thin to be bending whatever it was
back into herself onto the seat privately tucking her sorrow
into the pleat of her waist when is it one masters that fold?

Sticky Fingers

When Hansel stuffed mother into the oven
he stuck to her dress. He was using his
stick fingers and his bad eyes. He'd forgotten
his reading glasses. He mistook her for
the witch. He got the story wrong
though the moment was right. It wasn't
his fault. He'd eaten part of the house.
He had sugar sickness. We've all had
sugar sickness. You put your hand
in the bag of marshmallows,
and you eat one white puff after another.
You can't stop. You start to tremble then.
Your fingers are sticky and you can't control
what they do. Your lips are like glue.
You forgot how sweet sweet could be. What
sweet could make you do. Bees follow your breath
around the yard and it makes you crazy.
You don't know if you should run or
stand still. They want to dip into your mouth.
They land on your lips buzzing,
and there you are, suddenly panicked—
all those wings on your teeth.
And there she is, bending over the stove.
That house with its candy corners.
Its sticky roof. That syrup dripping off
the table. We've all read the story.
We all know what to do when push comes to shove.

Fungible Facts

Might as well water the stone.
The sidewalk. The snails. Wet down
the broken concrete. See if it might grow.
Water the sand. I never understood
why my baby daughter would drop
face down in the sand, press her mouth
into it. Take bites. She'd slip
from my hands, creep off the blanket.
She needed it. She needed
to put her tongue into it, swallow it
down. A baby in need of grit.
Like she knew something already.
They say this about babies.
Omniscient but they can't talk yet.
If you were to believe we eat according
to what the body needs.
Chocolate. Potato Chips. Smoke.
Something the body is missing.
It wants to balance itself
the way water wants to run to the sea.
Like watering the hole out of which
you just pulled the rose.
You forget which thing needs watering.
Which thing to forget.

A Kind of Ruffling Course in the World

after Nathaniel Philbrick, Mayflower

It was a strange, alarming, confusing performance.
They forsook their houses, living in swamps
and other desert places; they were not the only ones
to have taken flight into the wilderness.

They forsook their houses, living in swamps
and other desert places. Terrified by the first glimpse
of the new world, they took flight into the wilderness;
everywhere they went they were stunned.

By the rivers of Babylon she wept, terrified by the glimpse
of that ship lingering in the harbor, inexplicably.
Everywhere they went they were stunned.
It was difficult to believe that anyone could be alive

for more than a week. The ship lingering inexplicably,
made with a rope of their own making.
It was difficult to believe that anyone could be alive,
overwhelmed by this naked and barren place

made with a rope of their own making.
They were not the only ones
overwhelmed by this naked and barren place.
It was a strange, alarming, confusing performance.

Distant Buffaloes

after Gail Boyajian

How you feel about any one thing at any given moment
   is a matter of perspective, the shortest distance
between two points, parallel lines intersecting

and the vanishing point something mathematical.
   You could draw it with your pencil. You can bend it.
As in this painting before me: hummingbirds

in the foreground gigantic, and distant buffaloes
   diminutive as cats, while the tornado
bearing down over the hill is no bigger

 than a blade of grass. Everything in the foreground
   unperturbed. Even the Robert Frost man in a brown suit
sitting on the log. He's looking right at us, his thick white hair

 glowing. Nothing to worry about, he seems to be saying,
   his back to the funnel dangling down like a rope—
like an umbilicus. Like a whip.

4444

It was a two-month rental and the phone number
an easy number to mistake. Those four fours in a row.
I want you back, someone whispered one morning
into my ear. *Congratulations!* another yelled
that afternoon. It was like being popular.
You could hear a shoe drop in the other room
it was otherwise so quiet in that house.
It was spring. I watched the ice go out
on the lake. Watched it pleat itself up on the shore.
It sounded like moaning. I was counting
manure wagons going by my house.
This was the country after all. The farm trucks
busy. Time to empty out the manure pit.
I know you have my wife! a man screamed in
my ear one night. *I'm coming to get her!*
I tried to tell him it was the wrong number
but he hung up before I could think what to say.
I thought maybe I'd forgotten something
like in those dreams you have where you've
done something you can't undo.
I found an earring down behind the wood stove, a sock
between the couch and the wall.
His name is Walt. He's out there driving around.
I have no idea what kind of car he drives,
but when I heard the motor boat banging
up and down on the lake outside, I ducked.
The aluminum hull like a flat metal palm.
I don't have to tell you: I'm worried.
The temporary nature of my circumstances is beginning to impress me.

Does That White Seem Cold?

Finally Dottie put her finger on the problem.
　　It seemed pleasant enough.
She had spent days counting heads
　　in the photos of protesting crowds.
She'd seen the six-foot wingspan,
　　what nature does to a family, something
deep inside us all. An unending
　　process of stopping and staring.
Poster children for existentialism,
　　weighted and rotund, the solid,
seated female nude
　　suddenly unsettled; caressing form
and contour, line and erasure.
　　Apples rush across a table, their
sense of becoming and dissolving
　　simultaneously. A bouquet of flowers
suggests a swarm of bees.
　　It seemed like work to drink it.

DNA

In my understanding DNA is like putty.
You can scrape cells off a pencil and into a cup.
Can tell who the person is. Who their kin is.
Where their kin went.
Which of the original 13 mothers they come from.
In my understanding of DNA you can bring
someone back. You take the cells. Add science.
Clone them. There you have it. A new person. A cow.
Small goat. Whatever you started with.
You could make it grow there.
You could take the toothpick out of the dead man's pocket.
Take the dead man's pocket. The last
suit he wore. The gold buttons on the suit.
Take the hair from the collar.
It's the dead man's genetic duplicate.
It would be like getting out of prison.
Your name cleared at last.
Like that man last week in Columbus.
In prison 25 years for a murder
he didn't do. DNA got him free.
Such a simple procedure.
Finally a mistake you can fix.
There he was on the front page of the paper.
Holding up the lucky penny he just found.
"Heads up!" he shouts out.
"It's my lucky day." His name is Howard.
That was Ohio. This is Indiana.
I have your shoes.
I have the papers you left on the desk.

Dreaming of Disguise

When I came upon the hair at the corner of Ovington and Fourth, I was relieved. I saw there was room for more. A disguise, some kind of getaway plan, the hair in dark mounds spilling out of garbage bags into the street. You could make a beard out of it and some coats. You could make someone new out of all that hair. A new man. A new you. People were stepping into the hair. There was no way to avoid it. There was a breeze and the shorn hair was blowing in it. The barber shop was closed and the men to whom the hair had once belonged were somewhere in the neighborhood. The women walked past with scarves on their heads, and the boys were wearing baseball caps.

Clearly there were some cold men walking around. Their heads shaved and the bags of hair split open on the sidewalk. I had hair on my feet. Hair stuck to the bottoms of my pant-legs. I had a plan. It is important in this life to have a plan. A course of action. This was intimacy, I thought to myself, the hair of your newly coiffed head drifting in piles on the street. Some of it getting onto the tires of cars. Some of it getting on the R train with the people it was clinging to. Something had been split open by mistake. I went into the post office to mail a letter and the postal clerk was cranky, could not change anything bigger than a five. We were in trouble there standing in that line, all of us with hair on our clothes, and myself thinking about possible disguises. About becoming a man made of hair. In plain view. Because this was a government agency and not just the corner grocery, the man behind the glass pane grumped at everybody, equally.

Auction

I have confused my mother with some acres. I have confused my
mother with a field of corn. My mother herself has become confused.
It is common knowledge. Time to sell but just what is being sold?
She was quiet. She was mum. She was mother. She worked. She sold herself.
Her teeth are bad now. She has a bad heart. The little battery in her chest keeps
her going. She refused the hearing aid. She confused it with a fork.
She has forgotten the dentist appointment. She forgot the dog and the dog ran
down the street after her. *One more time,* the dog pound people said,
and the dog stays here. The dog bites people when they try to move her too fast.
Not much you could get for that dog. And the kitchen table funky.
Her sons walk through the kitchen with their boots on. She makes good ice
tea but she has forgotten her dinner in the back of the fridge.
There it is, last week's uneaten meat. Tuesday's vegetables.

Silage

Selling the farm is not the same as buying the farm.
Buying the farm means you die. Selling the farm
means someone else died. Someone died and left
you it. It's not easy selling a farm. There's the mound of
shit you can't move. The bones of the farm animals
dragged off into the upper pasture. Here's some teeth.
Here's a thigh bone. Here's the pelvis. Big enough
to make a house out of almost. The cows lumbering
across the acreage and the problematic mother
refusing to move. It's like selling something you
can't get your hands on really though it's big and
it smells bad. What to do with the grass silage
fermenting? What to do with the turkey buzzards still
circling that field where the cows give birth?
What to do with the calf just now coming out
of the cow? The calf lands on the ground in a splash
of bone; flies land on her eyes. On her new mouth.
Nothing you can do about the flies. Meanwhile Mother
is sitting in Father's vacant chair. She is deciding not to
go anywhere. She doesn't want to sell the farm
though it's not up to her any longer.
"So it goes," she says. "This is the last calf," Brother
says. You take pictures. You stare at that
calf on the ground. How hot the sun is you think.
How still the air. How loud those birds are
in the trees. That massive flock of starlings.

Plank by Plank

Moon looks at it. The pine boughs. Lake. And what you
    never had and/or what you walked away from, or
what was given to you but you lost. If you

lost your place in line. What you failed to do. What doesn't happen.
    Builds itself in the moonlight plank by plank. Nail-gun poised, the new windows
placed. What you gave up. What you got rid of, what you

never had. Misplaced. You could go over to that building
    fixing itself in the moonlight and look out those windows
as if looking out the eyes of yourself already dead. As days are. As what

you left behind is. As if capable of doing that, of dying
    and coming back into the building that was yourself and looking out.
How white the planks are in the moonlight building themselves.

What you lost making its own little house with its new windows.
    If there was a chair there you could go sit in it. You could listen
to the animals moving tree to tree, the forest shifting toward you.

It makes a sound by itself. The new planks adjusting themselves
    around the nails. The shine of the nails in the moonlight. And those
new windows. What you didn't do. What you couldn't keep. What

you walked away from. That structure it makes of itself.
    That shrine. Everything precise. The little village a house is.
Some planks. A forest.

Tuck & Roll

The people on my hill tuck & roll
out their back doors and like hula hoops swoop
downhill to the bay where the boats wait.
The contentious children who live at the foot of the hill
are selling tickets but everyone forgot their money.
They have printed out the tickets on their homework assignments
and one of them is accusing the other of copying.
Standing on the bank, digging in his pocket, one
man declares there's a problem with The Evolution.
The beavers have eaten all the trees around
the lake; they want to know what to do next.
"These are interesting times," everyone says,
getting onto the makeshift boats
made out of tractor trailer trucks with pontoons
for wheels. We're going somewhere and we seem
to have been going there the whole time.
It's a strange panic we're in but the water
calms us. The light, the sound of the waves,
the fish that none of us can identify jumping
in and out of the hull. The children who sold
the tickets in the first place are back on the shore
waving the papers in their hands. Shouting.
We can see their mouths opening and closing,
see them jumping up and down. It seems they
meant to come with us but were a bit busy
printing up the tickets in the backyard,
squabbling about which one of them would
hold the revenues. *Sorry*, a man shrugs from
the deck. "Better luck next time," his girlfriend
shouts. "See you later, alligators!"

Spikehorn

Dead on the ice a week now, spikehorn buck half-
eaten, torn up, and the neighborhood dogs delighting
in it. Running off to roll in it. Pull at it. Like they were
something feral. Tough as the coyotes that yanked it
down in the first place. Mine comes back with blood on his snout.
Scolded, he lies down on the rug. Stink on his fur.
Dog that lies on my bed, sleeps on my couch.
Licks my hands with such tenderness. Dog that goes
with me everywhere. I can smell him across the room.
Fresh meat in his belly. His gut gurgling. So this morning,
I went out on the ice, gathered it up: hide, hooves, the head
still attached by spinal column but everything in between
eaten out. I scooped it into the blue recycle box, ribs
half-chewed, sticking up at me, frozen eye open; I
took it away in the car. Laid it down in the woods a mile
from here. The way you do when you have a wild pet
that needs to be freed. Or creatures you don't want in the yard.
Something you don't want to kill but you don't want it
in your garbage can, or up on the porch staring in at you.
You take them far away and leave them. Hope
they won't find their way back but there's always that story of
some plucky something traveling 150 miles and ending up on the door-
step scratching at the screen. How surprised the family is when it
reappears; they brag about its intelligence. Such loyalty.
I took the carcass far up the road where my dog won't be dragging it back here.
That he will be done with it and the neighbor's dog
be done with it. Which is what we do with the dead.
We hope they stay where they are; and if they come back
we want them to only come back in one piece.
Glossy hair. Soft, rounded bellies and eyes that look back at us.
Not ruined. And the stories they never told returning with them.
That they will sit down and tell us what they never told us.
The unfinished parts. When they come back.
That they will breathe back the breath they took from the room when they left us.
They will give it back. What they took. When they come back.

IV

The Miss Nancy Papers

1.

On the day I decided I'd let "bygones be bygones"
having counted up some significant "bygones," I, of course
felt suddenly relieved. I was driving south towards
some of the places I'd done some things wrong in
and vice versa been done to. My dog was too damn
hot. He was panting over my shoulder. Drops of water
fell off his tongue onto my arm. "Go sit down," I told him.
It was as if he was asking over and over if we
were there yet. I wasn't there yet. With my list.
The bygones. I was never what Romper Room termed
a "Do-Bee" and neither did I like the Mouseketeers
Club. That indefatigable cheerfulness. Every one of those kids
a Do-Bee. No match touchers. No car stander uppers.
No street players. Miss Nancy liked them.

2.

Miss Nancy liked them. Those kids that could claim
they were Do-Bees and never did anything wrong. They were
plate cleaners. Not food fussys. They didn't throw up
in the car. They didn't stand on the seat like my dog's
doing right now, trying to climb into the front because
it's too hot or he has to pee or he hates this damn highway.
We slow down for the construction zones, afraid of tickets
at all times. The Do-Bees getting the Don't-Bees though
we know it's never that simple. In my new mode, I try to resist
reductionism, something I was accused of by a certain scholar
in college English class. I had the answers it seemed
for just about everything, but the logic was rather skewed.
Slowing down makes the dog think that we're about to
stop. Go for a swim, a little run by the river. Have some fun.

3.

He thinks we're about to stop. Go for a swim, a little run
by the river. If dogs think in anything but the five senses.
Heat. Shiny water. Birds clucking. And the little stinks
other animals leave behind that we humans just can't smell.
He has a nose for it; finds the carcass and rolls in it, the way I,
in my unreformed self of half an hour ago, have often rolled
in my own or others' muck. "No more!" I say. Out they go,
my bad inclinations. No more being mad at the dead.
What anyone did or didn't do; who said what to whom.
Zip it up. Toss it out the window. Watch it bounce
down the highway behind you. Just like in the old days.
When we chucked trash out of cars. Before seat-belts.
A few short years after Sputnik. A car load of Don't-Bees.
Kids standing on the back seat. Dad smoking at the wheel.

4.

Dad smoking at the wheel. None of us kids with any idea
where any of us might go. Some kind of blank bouncing
around in the back seat. Match touchers. Street players.
I'd like to say I never did anything wrong though I
once shot an elastic band into Brian Hoyt's face.
By mistake of course. The teacher himself quit teaching
that year. Something about the way we refused
to assemble for him. We practiced fainting at recess.
You can make yourself black out, crash to the floor.
This was the countryside. Small town America.
We were already restless and the teachers threatening us
with the Russians. Bald Khrushchev banging the UN table
with his shoe. Franco was alive and well.
My brothers called me Butch though I'm not really butch.

5.

I'm not really butch and neither is the dog in the back seat
who has finally lain down and is licking his privates.
How do you know where it all first assembles? One block
of yourself at a time. Miss Nancy showed everybody how
to wash our hands but most of us were grubby anyway.
"Que sera, sera," mother sang in the front seat knitting,
tiny wrappers flying out as we drove. Spilled milk.
Water over a dam. I'm letting bygones be gone. Adios.
Ciao. Like a ring that flies off your finger into the sea.
Not much you can do about it. I wasn't a "food fussy"
but it's never a good idea to eat or smoke something
just because someone offers it. "Hash, acid, pot," the street
people whispered to us as we passed. So we made some
bad choices. Left some places we shouldn't have.

6.

Left some places we shouldn't have. Stayed when we
should have left. Got happy. Went broke. Got confused.
Talking about my generation. We threw rocks at cop cars.
Got gassed in public squares. Smashed some bank windows.
Deserted. Refused to go. Dressed like ladies when we went
into the draft board. Back when they wouldn't take you
if you were queer. You could lose your children too.
Get fired. "Do Bee a plate cleaner," Miss Nancy and her man
helper sang in their grown-up voices. Don't be a job leaver.
A retirement plan leaver. Do-Bees know there's nothing grand
in store for them. They don't leave their names in public places.
Their dogs don't stink. They fall in love with people that will do them
some good. "I'm a Do-Bee all day long," they sang at us.
There was indeed some finger-wagging we needed to pay attention to.

7.

Some finger-wagging we needed to pay attention to though
we mocked it. "Don't Bee a street player," they sang in their
know-it-all voices to the children glaring back at the sets. They
suspected all of us. Match touchers smoking father's cigarettes
in the cornfield. Lighting little fires with magnifying glasses.
Stealing cookies. Chalking up the stuff that pissed us off.
Things didn't roll off our backs though we swept plenty of it
under the rug. We kept tallies. If I could wrap it up now.
Bury it like we buried my mother last month. Said some prayers.
Sang some songs. Walked away from each other. A Do-Bee
doesn't say what she needs to say because she's a safe player,
Miss Nancy sang. She is not a shouter or a stomper.
She doesn't look back and moan about mistakes she made.
She didn't make them. She is so much prettier when she smiles.

8.

Made some mistakes, but I'm smiling at you now. My reformed
self. I threw that crap from the car. Got rid of it that day.
What I did to whom, and who did it to me. That dog I left
with my ex. Three cats. "Blue skies, nothing but blue skies,"
my mother liked to sing. The house I sold. Then the other.
The girlfriends that stalked me. How nervous I made them.
A Don't-Bee. Of course attracted to other Don't-Bees.
All of us up to no good. Day dreaming. Not following directions.
My dog and I were passing through one more "Watch for Moose"
section of the highway. We were burning up in the car. I was
thinking hard. Dog needed to get out so we stopped at the river.
When the flood came last month it emptied the cemetery,
scattered bodies downriver along with the houses that fell
into it. How we love a babbling brook, a lively little stream.

9.

Waterfront we call it. The babbling brook that washed the cemetery
downstream. Bits and pieces scattered along banks. A skull in a tree.
But it's gone now. Gathered up. Someone putting the bones back
together as we speak. Trying to identify the remains. My dog leaps
into the water. Takes a good long drink. He doesn't have to think
about what to do next. He does what he does and he wallows in it.
I would like to say that I myself have given up wallowing in it
as in wallowing in "sloughs of despond" which is something a Do-Bee
wouldn't do and doesn't have in the first place. What's done is done,
my mother liked to say. Miss Nancy knew about children like me,
itching and wiggling on the other side of the screen. Making faces.
Standing up in cars. Street players. My wet dog bounds back to me
happy. It's easy for him: sad to glad. One minute perturbed,
and the next, everything perfectly fine. Nothing to it.

10.

Everything perfectly fine. Something chummy about it,
and barely plausible. I'd like to say I know what I'm
doing here and why I did what I did. Some say what they need
to say when they need to say it. None of this squirrelly stuff.
Scribbling it down in secret. Holding the pages up to your face
in the dark. Sniffing the ink. Then hiding it somewhere
no one will see. There you are lying awake next to your
lover. You can't sleep. You climb quietly from the bed.
You get in your car and drive. This highway is familiar,
but the trees seem to have migrated. We pass into the state
I left and never should have: "Welcome home troops," it says.
"Massachusetts Welcomes You." Miss Nancy would salute
if she were here in the car. If there were a parade.
If anyone could figure out what war we were coming home from.

11.

If anyone could figure out what war we were coming home from
we would come home from it. Or why we were there
in the first place. My mother made me wear white gloves
when we went to the city. She sewed up my coat pockets
so I couldn't put my hands in them, shove them out of shape.
One afternoon riding the train uptown with her, I popped
a coin in my mouth. I can still taste it on my tongue.
Back when dirty was dirty. The Towers had not yet been built.
This dog panting at my shoulder had of course not been
born, nor my daughter who came up out of the PATH train
to see the North Tower on fire, then all of it falling down.
I was 19 when I had her. College dropout, hippie,
war protestor. "Love it or leave it!" people shouted.
It didn't seem like a good idea to bring a child into the world.

12.

It didn't seem like a good idea to bring a child into it. What she's seen
since then. We watched that footage over and over as if no one
would believe it without seeing it three thousand times then some more.
You could play it back and watch everything return to its place.
When my daughter was born it seemed like something broken
had been fixed and given back to me. I can taste that coin in my mouth.
Feel my mother's hand at my lips. "Spit it out, now," she said, as firm
as Miss Nancy in all things. As firm as I try to be with my dog
when he refuses to do what he's supposed to do no matter what.
Here's the familiar exits on the highway. Places I lived and the love
I was in when I lived there. When my mother was dying, I held my
hand to her head, did my best to remember the Lord's prayer, not
having said it in a long time. I remembered the part about trespassing
and delivering us from evil, but what about temptation?

13.

What about temptation? Some have substituted trespass for debt
as if the two were intertwined. I told her I was sorry for what
I did or didn't do. What I didn't forget. That table I wouldn't set.
The nurse dabbed some morphine on my mother's
tongue, "To ease the breathing," she said. I wasn't prepared.
There's nothing quiet about dying. It's like birth, but
backwards, the body banging against a door that won't open.
"Tanking" is what the nurse called it. Those last minutes.
Supposedly they can hear us, so I kept on talking but she
surprised me. Took a breath; then she stopped.
Took it with her and everything she never said along with it.
Which is how it's supposed to be, one of us
after the other seeing what there is to see and then going on
about our business letting bygones be bygones. Forget about it.

14.

Forget about it. Bygones are bygones. Like that day my dog
rolled in the dead fish, came back to me smiling and stinking,
scales and bits of bone stuck in his hair. I scolded him, sent him
to the cellar. It didn't last long. His shame. Nothing to it.
Perhaps it was that paper napkin flying out my window
made me think of Miss Nancy and her Du-Bees never doing
anything wrong, or it was just the direction I was driving in,
and the river we stopped by. How fast the flood came.
Towns cut off. Anxious calls from out of the area: "Have you seen
my mother, sister, father?" We look at the rivers running
through here a bit differently now. Even the one I paddled
with Nina. Out too late, it was darkroom dark, but for the camp
fire on the island above the bridge. We could hear someone singing.
That kind of night. The water broad and slow. Our voices hushed.

15.

No street players. No car stander uppers. Miss Nancy liked them.
Unlike this dog who thinks it's time to stop the car, go for a swim.
He's panting like a batch of kids standing on the back seat. "Lie down,"
I growl in my best butch voice though I'm not really butch. And yes,
I made some bad choices. Left some places I shouldn't have. Perhaps
there was some finger-wagging we ought to have paid attention to.
A Do-Bee doesn't make mistakes. So much prettier when she smiles—
she's smiling at you now. How we love a babbling brook, a lively little
stream; everything perfectly fine! Nothing to it. We would come home,
if anyone could figure out what war we were coming home from.
It didn't seem like a good idea to bring a child into it. As my mother
was dying, I remembered about trespassing and forgiving those who
trespass against us, but what do we do when we see what there is to see?
It was that kind of night. The water broad and slow. Our voices hushed.

"Do Bee a Do Bee" was the theme song from the television series Romper Room.
Miss Nancy was the hostess from 1958 to 1969.

Acknowledgments

Some of the poems in this book were originally published in *AGNI Online, Bloodroot, Calyx, FIELD, The Gay & Lesbian Review, Hanging Loose, The Journal, Lambda Literary Review, The New Review of Literature, Open Field, OR: A Literary Tabloid, Poemeleon, Prairie Schooner, Rhino, River Styx, Sinister Wisdom, Switched-on Gutenberg,* and *Tupelo Quarterly.*

With tremendous gratitude and love for their insightful, inspired, generous readings of many of these poems to Annie Boutelle, Ellen Doré Watson, Amy Dryansky, Maya Janson, Mary Koncel, and Diana Gordon—my po-group, the brilliant and delightful choco-vinas. You helped this book happen.

Thank you Maureen Conroy and Tekla McInerney for your love, your wit, and your hospitality—for making it possible for me to attend said po-group, and to Meme English, Paula Sayword, Judith Branzburg, Amy Ryan, and my sister Diana Hill for their continuing and enthusiastic support over these years.

And more gratitude and love to Jessamc, Amy, Max, Theo, and Zoey, whose laughter and support and joyful imaginings rekindle the world.

Finally, my appreciation to *FIELD*, and to Oberlin College Press, and especially to editors David Walker and David Young—thank you.

The FIELD Poetry Series

1993   Dennis Schmitz, *About Night: Selected and New Poems*
        Marianne Boruch, *Moss Burning*

1994   Russell Edson, *The Tunnel: Selected Poems*

1996   Killarney Clary, *By Common Salt*

1997   Marianne Boruch, *A Stick That Breaks and Breaks*

1998   Jon Loomis, *Vanitas Motel*
        Franz Wright, *Ill Lit: Selected & New Poems*

1999   Marcia Southwick, *A Saturday Night at the Flying Dog and Other Poems*

2000   Timothy Kelly, *Stronger*

2001   Ralph Burns, *Ghost Notes*
        Jon Loomis, *The Pleasure Principle*

2002   Angie Estes, *Voice-Over*
        Tom Andrews, *Random Symmetries: The Collected Poems of Tom Andrews*

2003   Carol Moldaw, *The Lightning Field*

2004   Marianne Boruch, *Poems: New & Selected*
        Jonah Winter, *Amnesia*

2005   Angie Estes, *Chez Nous*
        Beckian Fritz Goldberg, *Lie Awake Lake*

2006   Jean Gallagher, *Stubborn*

2007   Mary Cornish, *Red Studio*

2008   J. W. Marshall, *Meaning a Cloud*
        Timothy Kelly, *The Extremities*

2009   Dennis Hinrichsen, *Kurosawa's Dog*
        Angie Estes, *Tryst*

2010   Amy Newlove Schroeder, *The Sleep Hotel*

2011   Timothy O'Keefe, *The Goodbye Town*

2012   Jean Gallagher, *Start*
        Mark Neely, *Beasts of the Hill*

2013   Mary Ann Samyn, *My Life in Heaven*
        Beckian Fritz Goldberg, *Egypt from Space*
        Angie Estes, *Enchantée*

2014   Bern Mulvey, *Deep Snow Country*
        Dennis Schmitz, *Animism*

2015   Carol Potter, *Some Slow Bees*
        Mark Neely, *Dirty Bomb*